Christmas Carols
FOR VIOLIN DUET & PIANO

ISBN 978-1-70517-716-7

HAL•LEONARD®

Visit Hal Leonard Online at
www.halleonard.com

World headquarters, contact:
Hal Leonard
7777 West Bluemound Road
Milwaukee, WI 53213
Email: info@halleonard.com

In Europe, contact:
Hal Leonard Europe Limited
1 Red Place
London, W1K 6PL
Email: info@halleonardeurope.com

In Australia, contact:
Hal Leonard Australia Pty. Ltd.
4 Lentara Court
Cheltenham, Victoria, 3192 Australia
Email: info@halleonard.com.au

CONTENTS

Angels We Have Heard on High

Traditional French Carol
Arranged by Joshua Parman

Away in a Manger

William J. Kirkpatrick
Adapted from an arrangement
by Christopher Ruck

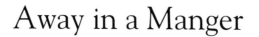

Deck the Hall

Traditional Welsh Carol
Arranged by Richard Walters

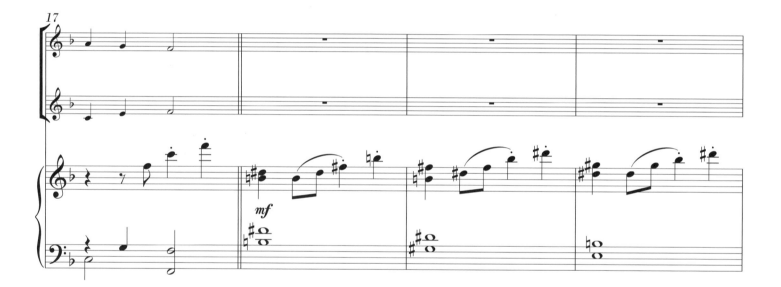

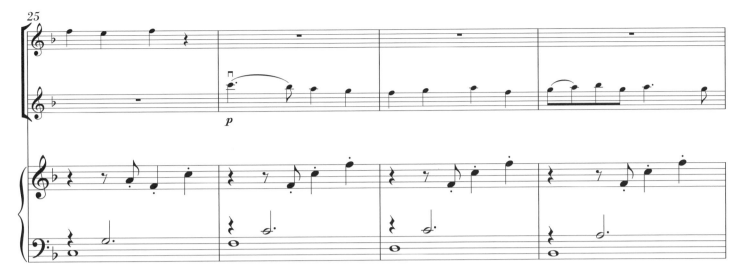

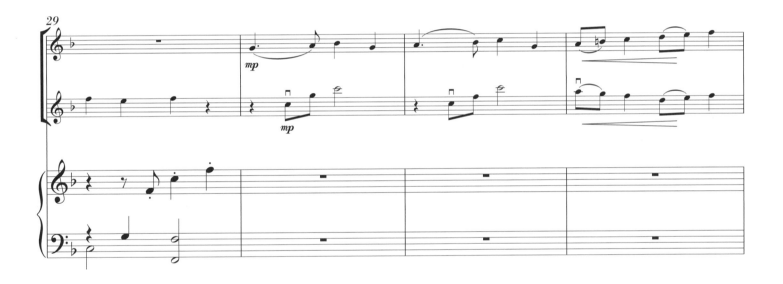

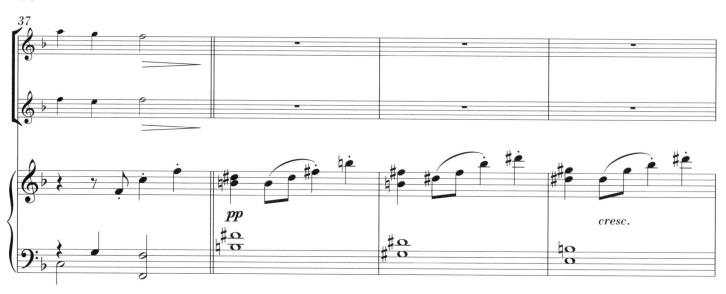

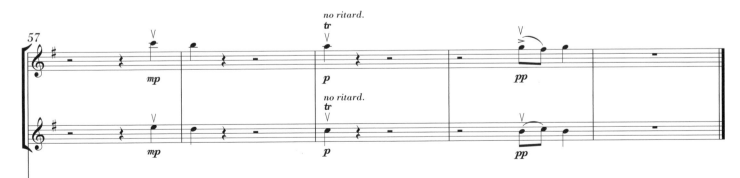

Coventry Carol

English Melody
Arranged by Joel K. Boyd

The First Noel

Traditional English Carol
Arranged by Joel K. Boyd

God Rest Ye Merry, Gentlemen

Traditional English Melody
Arranged by Brendan Fox

Slightly slower

In dulci jubilo

German Carol, 14th century
Arranged by Richard Walters

In the Bleak Midwinter

Gustav Holst
Adapted from an arrangement
by Brian Dean

Infant Holy, Infant Lowly

Polish Carol
Adapted from an arrangement
by Christopher Ruck

Slower

Joy to the World

George Frideric Handel
Arranged by Brendan Fox

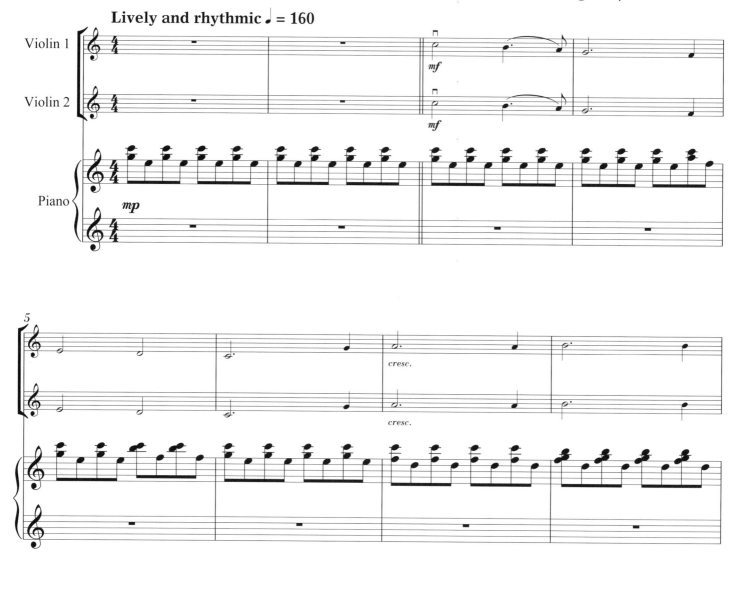

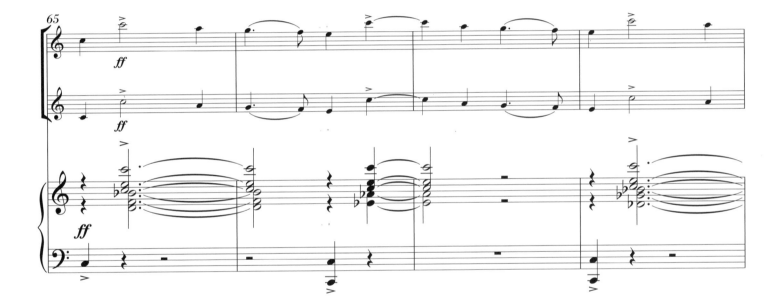

Lo, How a Rose E'er Blooming

Traditional German Carol
From *Kölner Gesangbuch*, 1599
Arranged by Richard Walters

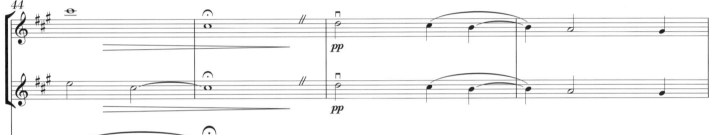

O Come, All Ye Faithful
(Adeste Fideles)

John Francis Wade
Arranged by Joshua Parman

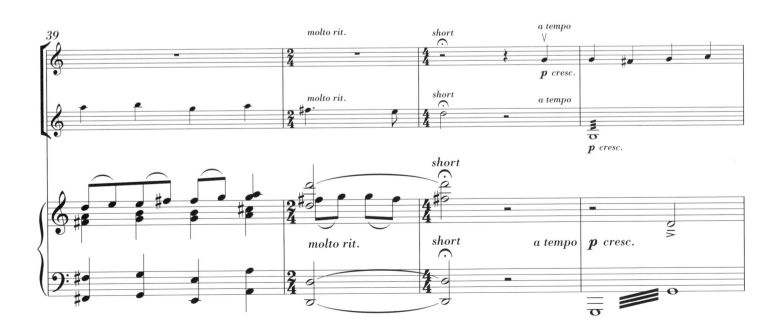

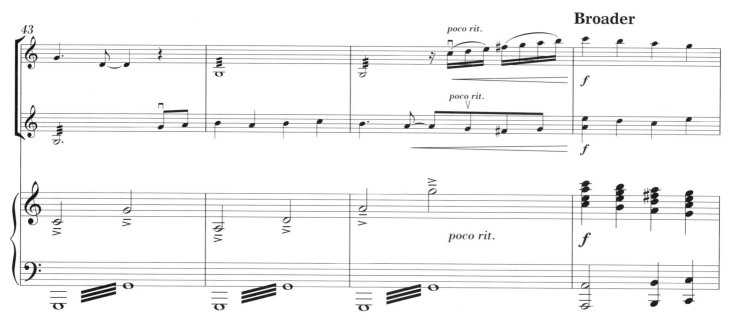

O Holy Night

Adolphe Adam
Transcribed by Celeste Avery

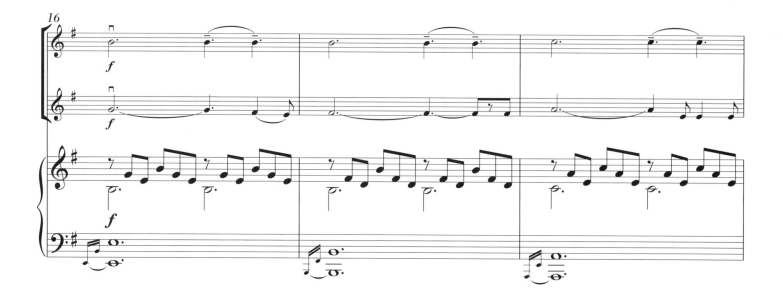

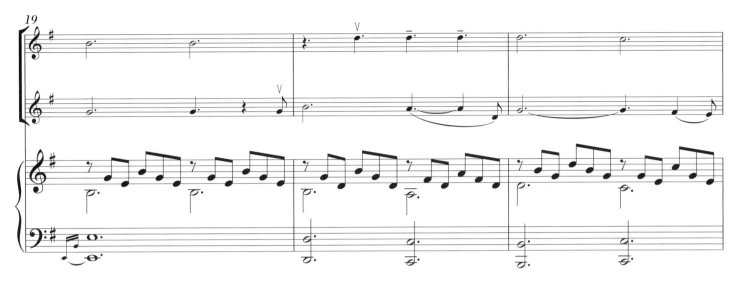

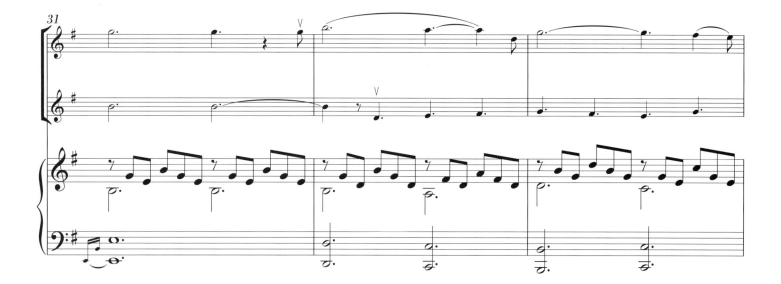

O Come, O Come Emmanuel

French Melody, 15th century
Arranged by Richard Walters

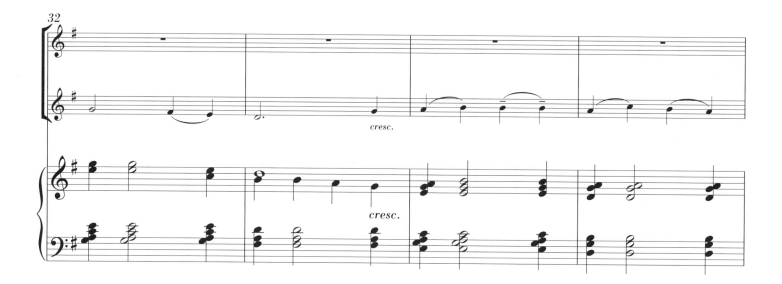

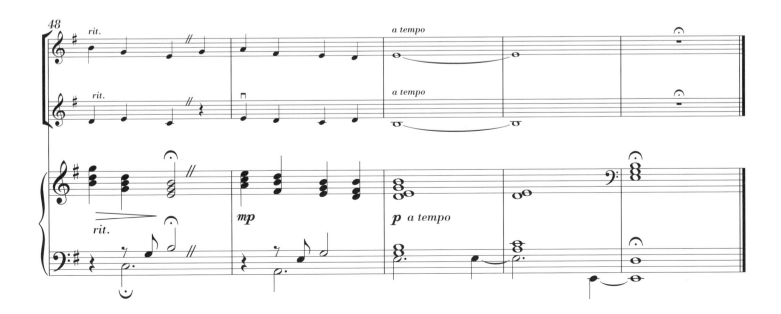

Still, Still, Still

Traditional Austrian Carol
Adapted from an arrangement
by Brian Dean

What Child Is This?

16th century English Folksong
Adapted from an arrangement
by Bryan Stanley

Andante con moto ♩. = 50-58

Silent Night

Franz X. Gruber
Arranged by Brendan Fox

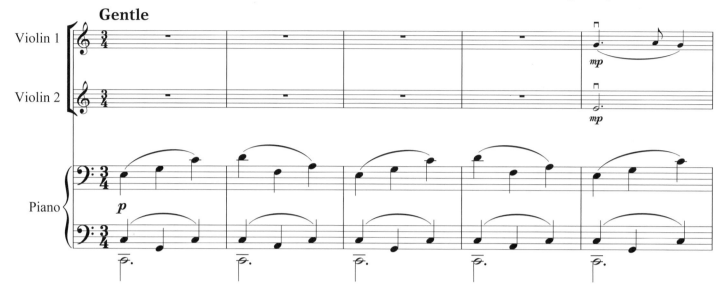

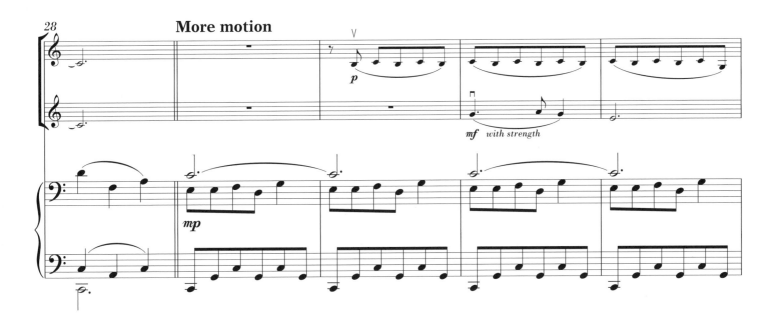

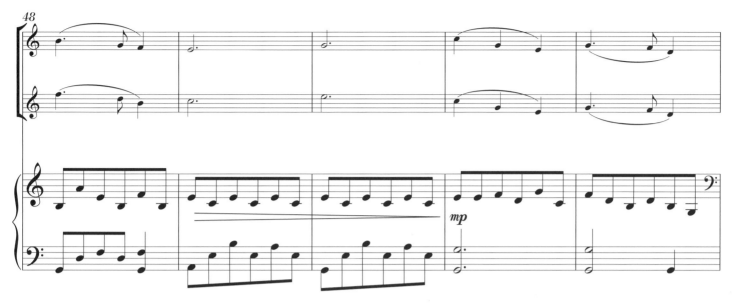

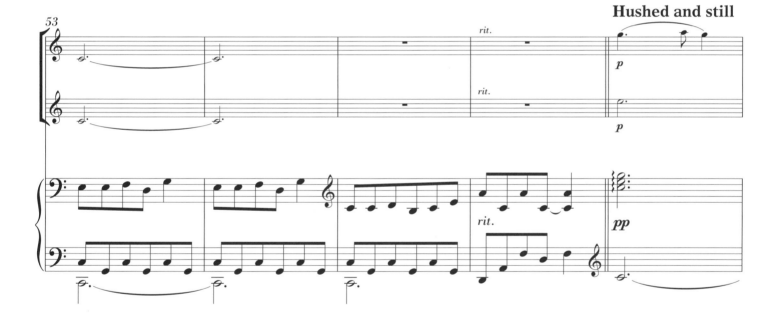

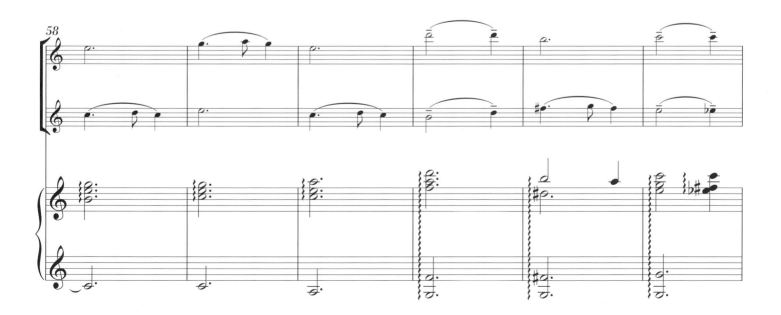

CONTENTS

Angels We Have Heard on High

Traditional French Carol
Arranged by Joshua Parman

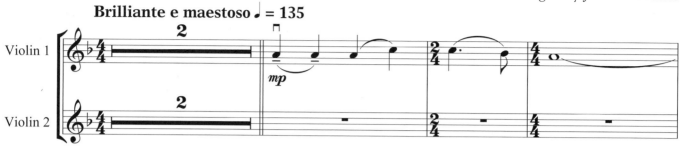

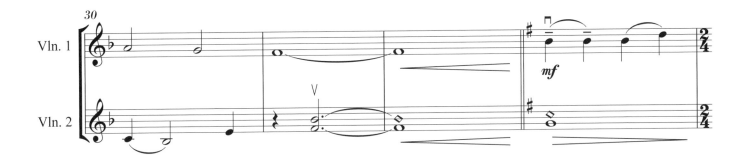

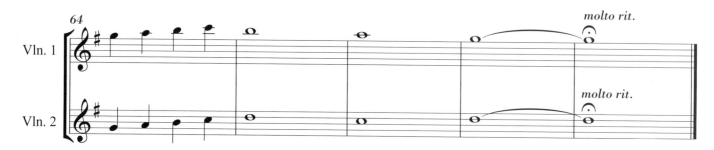

Joy to the World

George Frideric Handel
Arranged by Brendan Fox

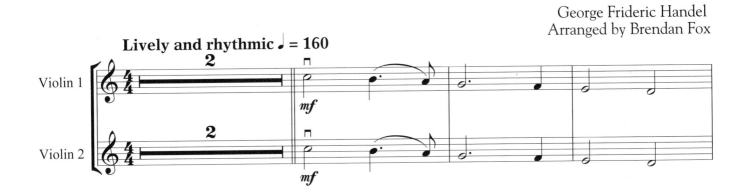

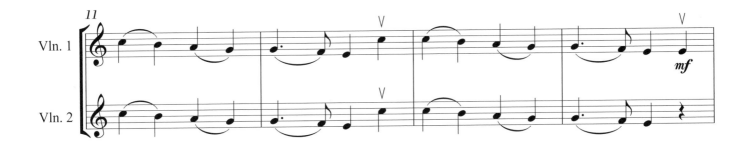

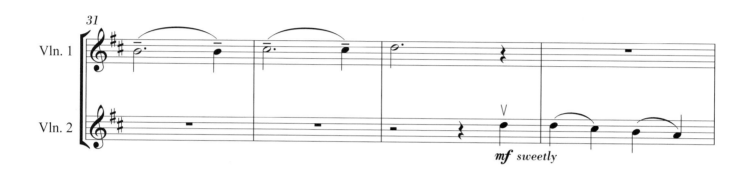

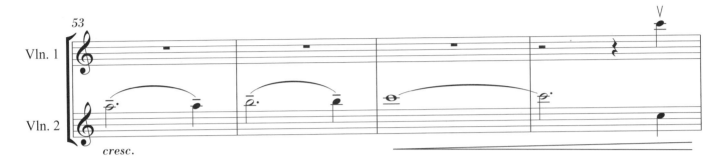

Away in a Manger

William J. Kirkpatrick
Adapted from an arrangement
by Christopher Ruck

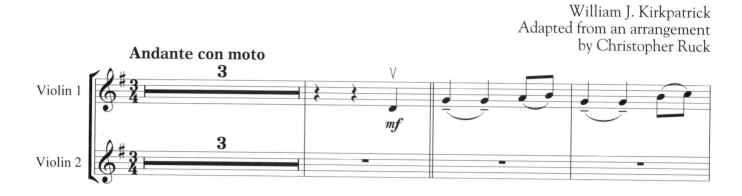

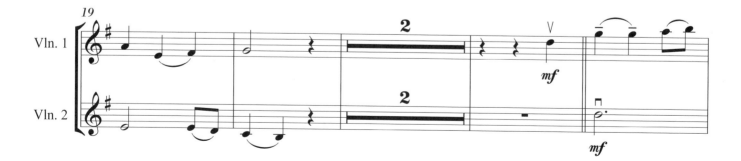

Coventry Carol

English Melody
Arranged by Joel K. Boyd

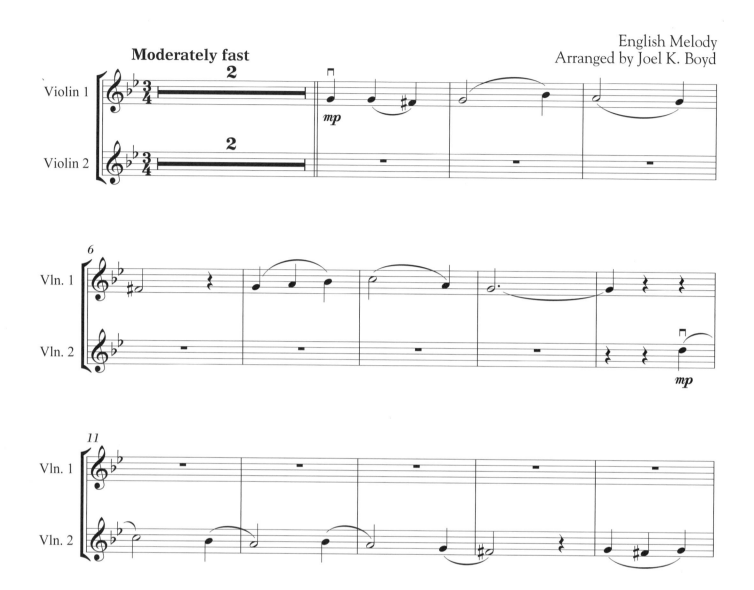

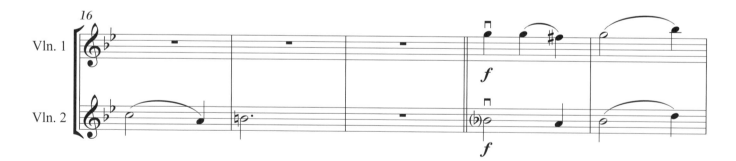

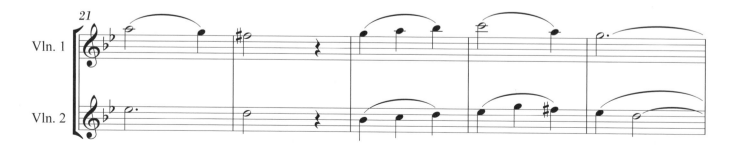

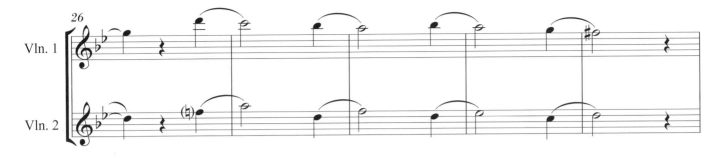

Deck the Hall

Traditional Welsh Carol
Arranged by Richard Walters

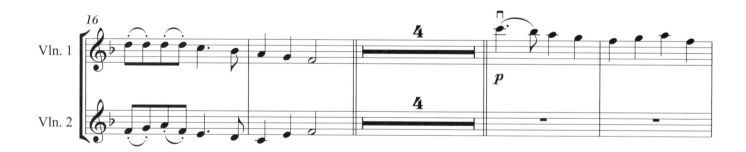

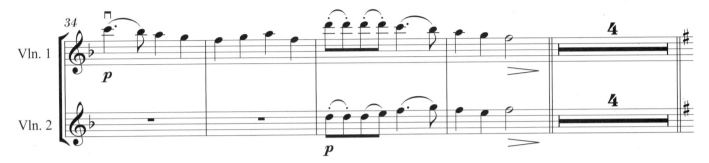

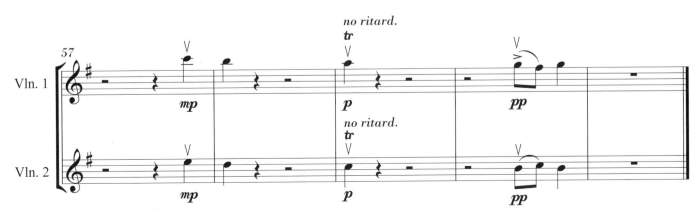

16

The First Noel

Traditional English Carol
Arranged by Joel K. Boyd

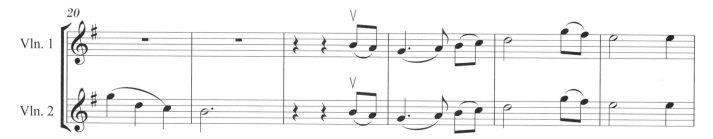

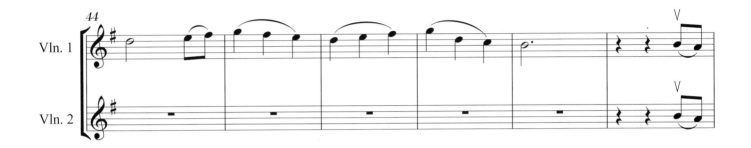

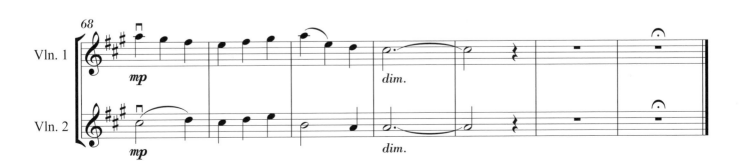

God Rest Ye Merry, Gentlemen

Traditional English Melody
Arranged by Brendan Fox

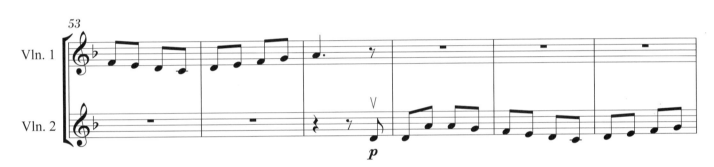

Slightly slower

In dulci jubilo

German Carol, 14th century
Arranged by Richard Walters

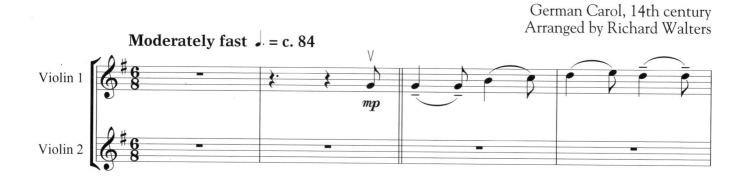

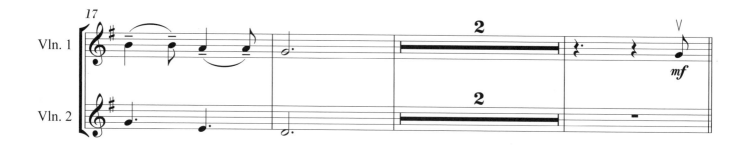

In the Bleak Midwinter

Gustav Holst
Adapted from an arrangement
by Brian Dean

Infant Holy, Infant Lowly

Polish Carol
Adapted from an arrangement
by Christopher Ruck

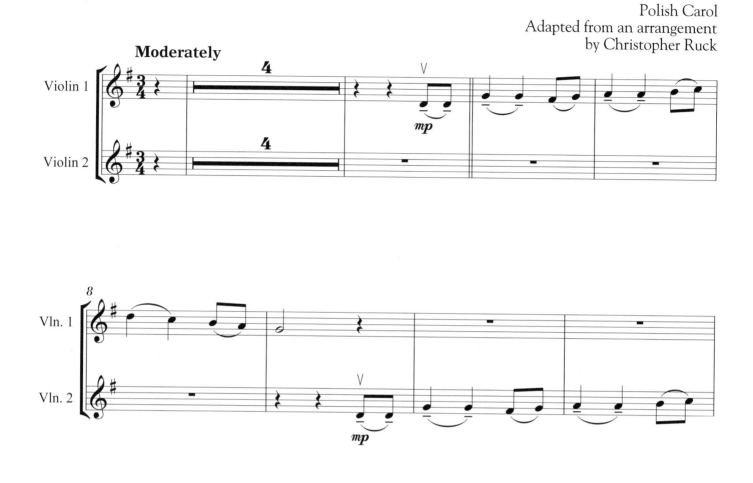

Lo, How a Rose E'er Blooming

Traditional German Carol
From *Kölner Gesangbuch*, 1599
Arranged by Richard Walters

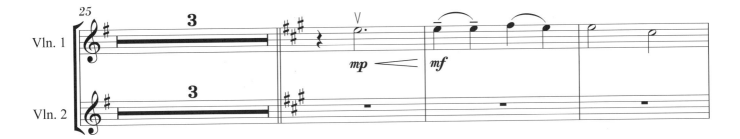

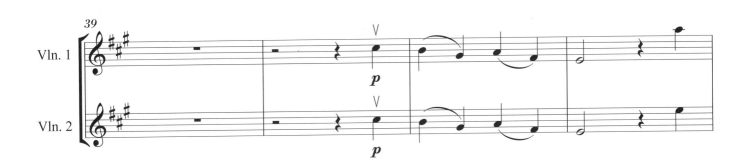

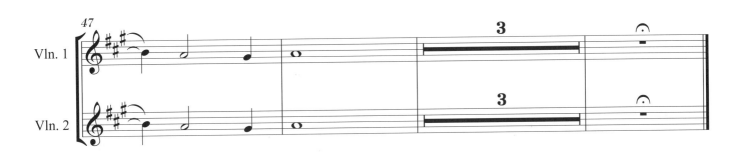

O Come, All Ye Faithful
(Adeste Fideles)

John Francis Wade
Arranged by Joshua Parman

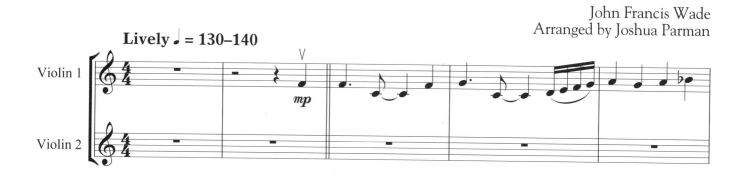

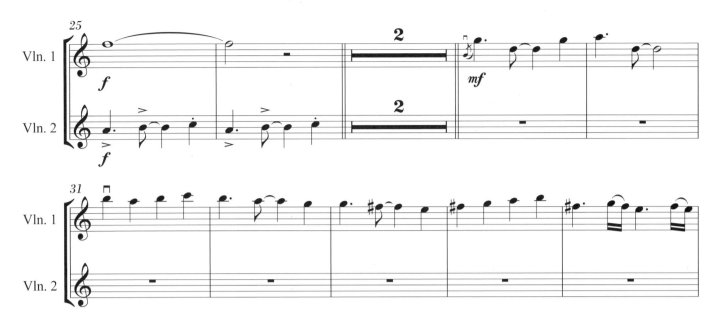

Broader

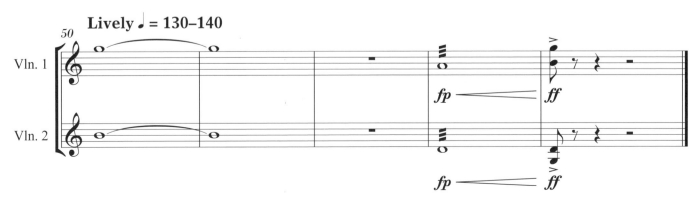

O Come, O Come Emmanuel

French Melody, 15th century
Arranged by Richard Walters

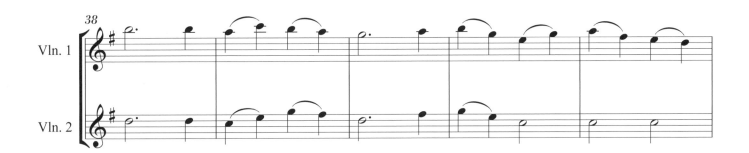

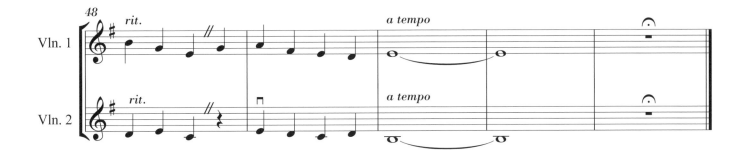

O Holy Night

Adolphe Adam
Transcribed by Celeste Avery

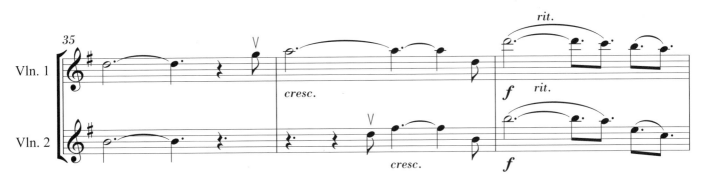

Still, Still, Still

Traditional Austrian Carol
Adapted from an arrangement
by Brian Dean

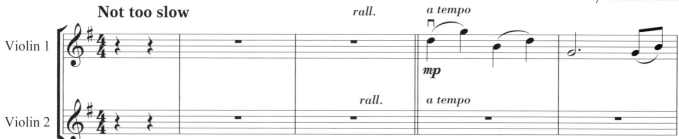

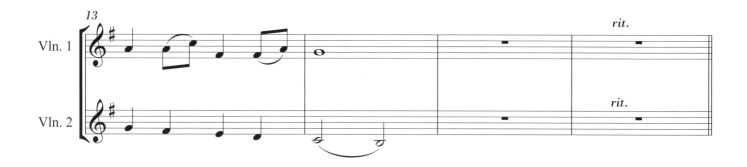

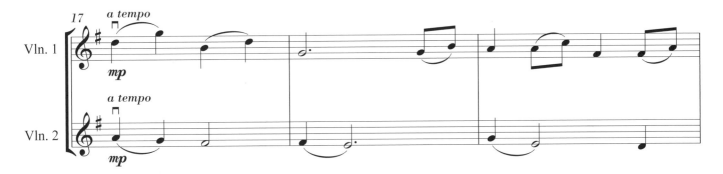

What Child Is This?

16th century English Folksong
Adapted from an arrangement
by Bryan Stanley

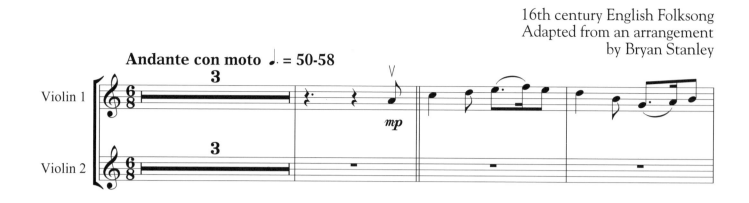

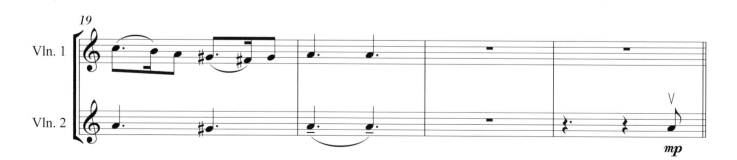

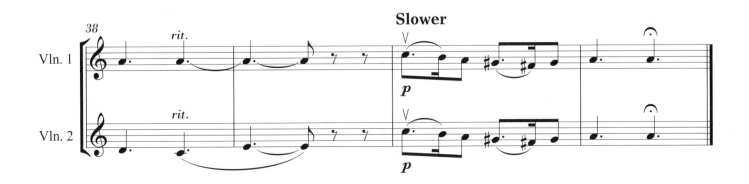

Silent Night

Franz X. Gruber
Arranged by Brendan Fox

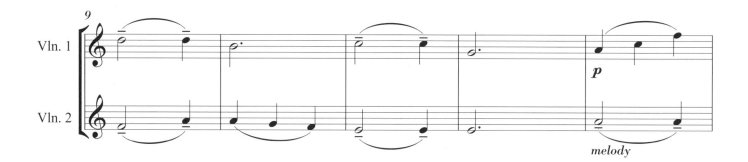

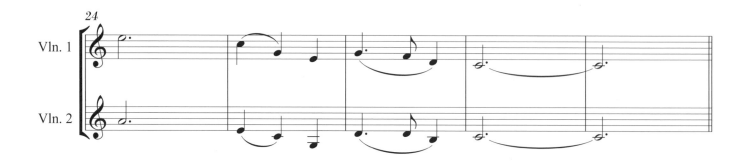

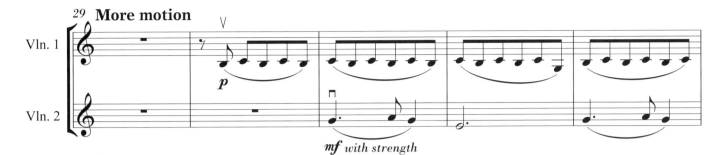

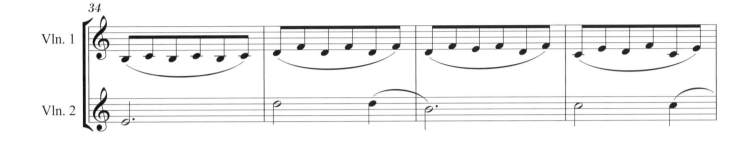

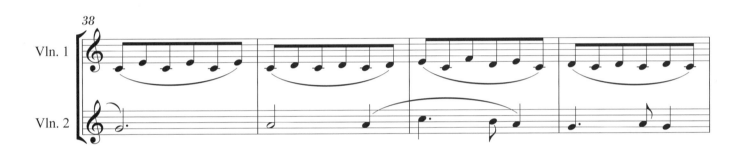

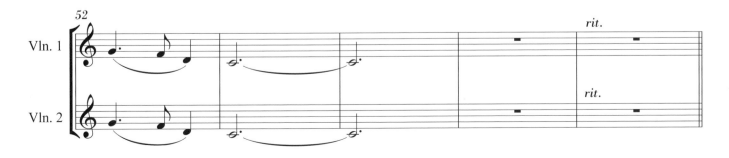

Hushed and still

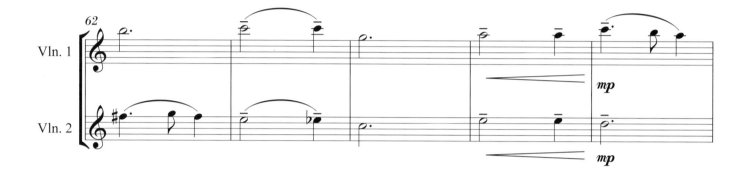

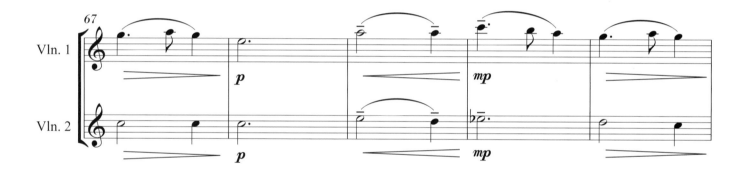

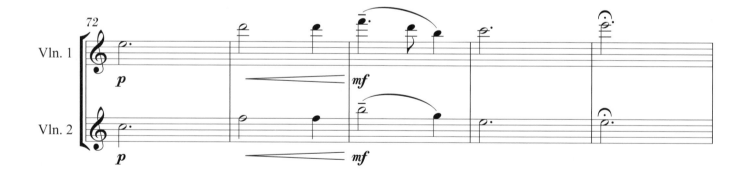

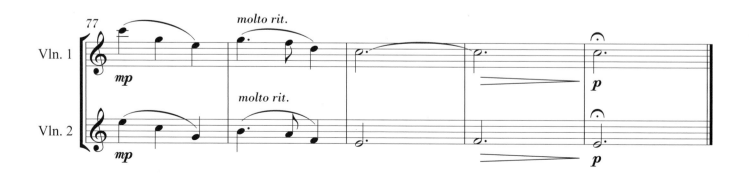

Christmas Carols
FOR VIOLIN DUET & PIANO

ISBN 978-1-70517-716-7

HAL•LEONARD®

Visit Hal Leonard Online at
www.halleonard.com

World headquarters, contact:
Hal Leonard
7777 West Bluemound Road
Milwaukee, WI 53213
Email: info@halleonard.com

In Europe, contact:
Hal Leonard Europe Limited
1 Red Place
London, W1K 6PL
Email: info@halleonardeurope.com

In Australia, contact:
Hal Leonard Australia Pty. Ltd.
4 Lentara Court
Cheltenham, Victoria, 3192 Australia
Email: info@halleonard.com.au

CONTENTS

Angels We Have Heard on High

Traditional French Carol
Arranged by Joshua Parman

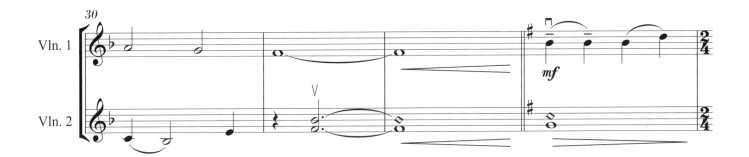

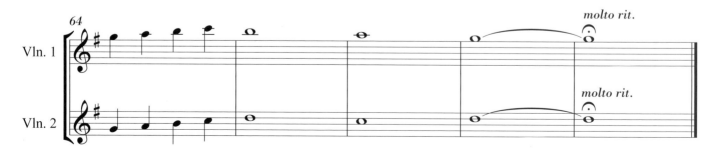

Joy to the World

George Frideric Handel
Arranged by Brendan Fox

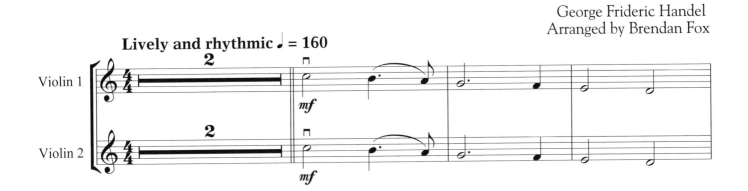

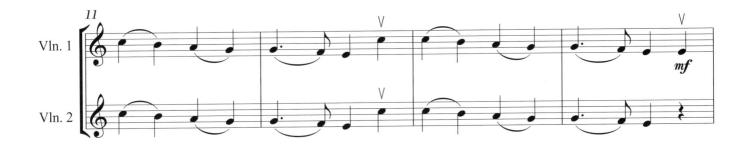

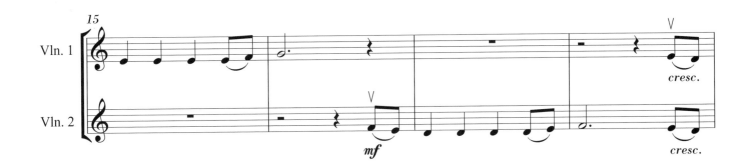

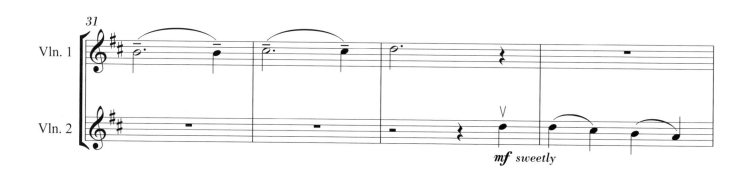

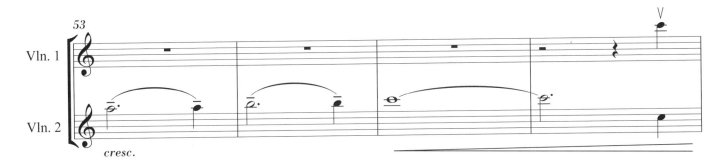

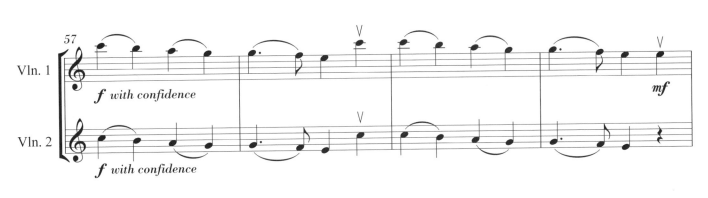

Away in a Manger

William J. Kirkpatrick
Adapted from an arrangement
by Christopher Ruck

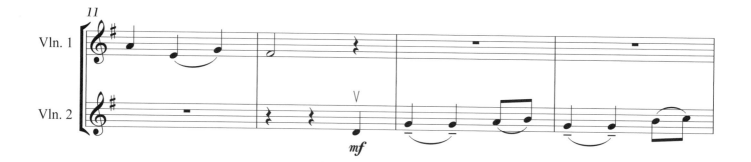

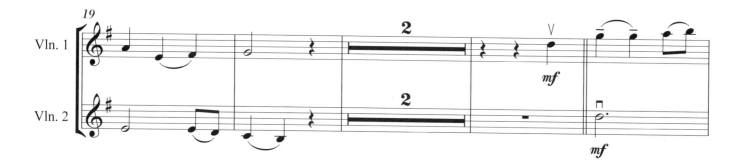

Coventry Carol

English Melody
Arranged by Joel K. Boyd

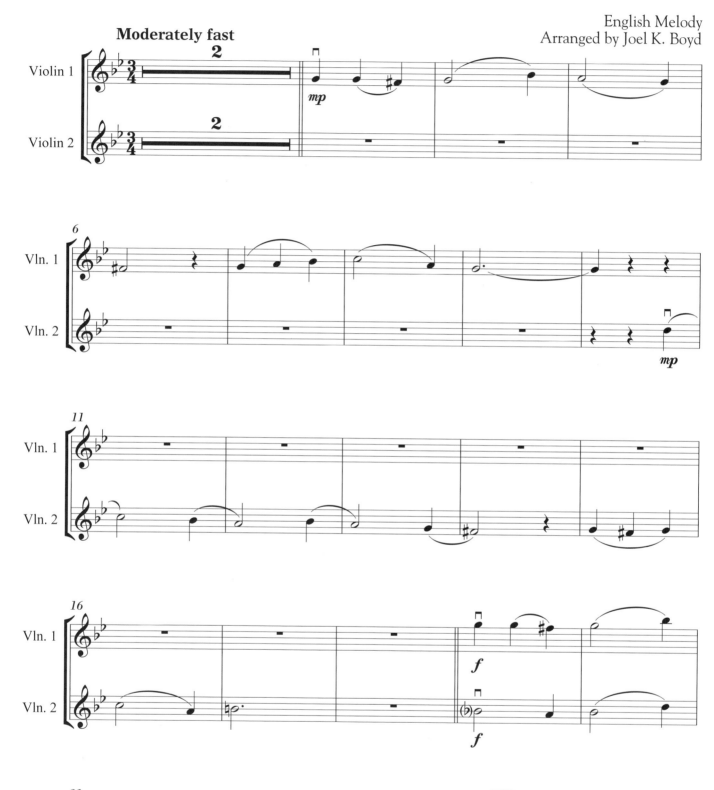

Deck the Hall

Traditional Welsh Carol
Arranged by Richard Walters

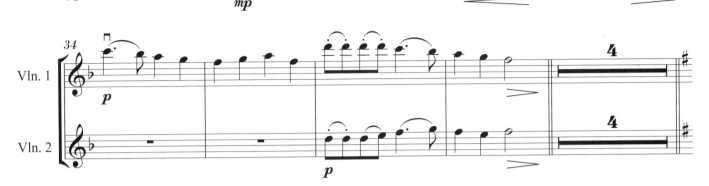

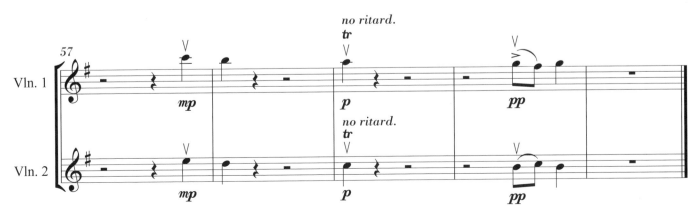

The First Noel

Traditional English Carol
Arranged by Joel K. Boyd

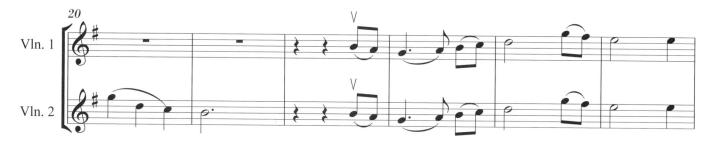

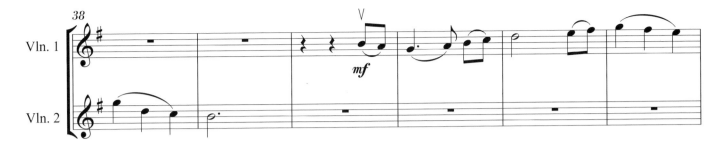

God Rest Ye Merry, Gentlemen

Traditional English Melody
Arranged by Brendan Fox

Slightly slower

In dulci jubilo

German Carol, 14th century
Arranged by Richard Walters

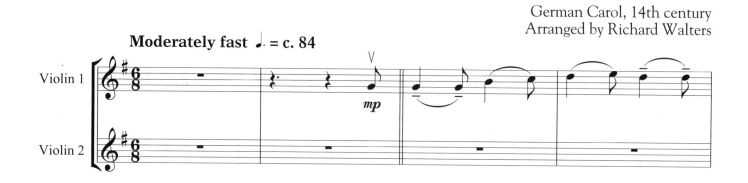

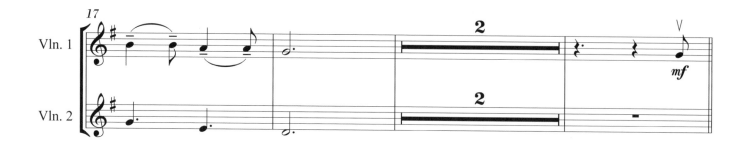

In the Bleak Midwinter

Gustav Holst
Adapted from an arrangement
by Brian Dean

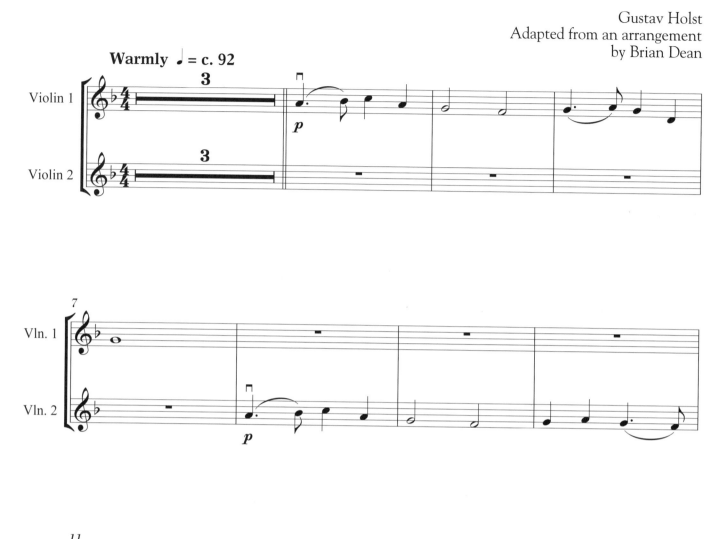

Infant Holy, Infant Lowly

Polish Carol
Adapted from an arrangement
by Christopher Ruck

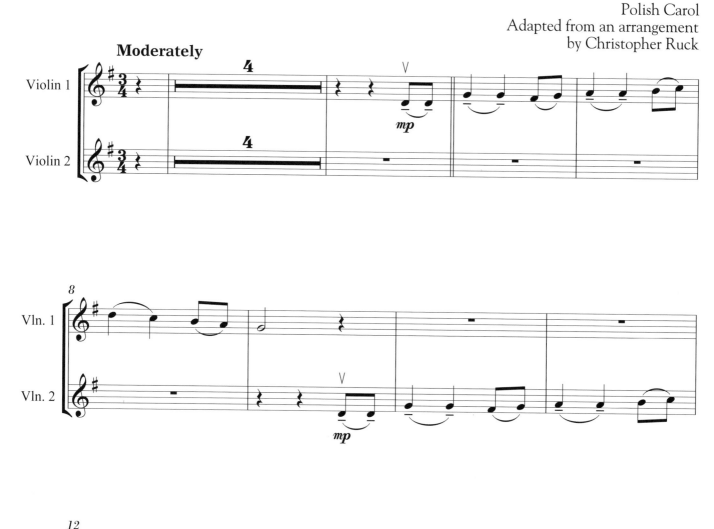

Lo, How a Rose E'er Blooming

Traditional German Carol
From *Kölner Gesangbuch*, 1599
Arranged by Richard Walters

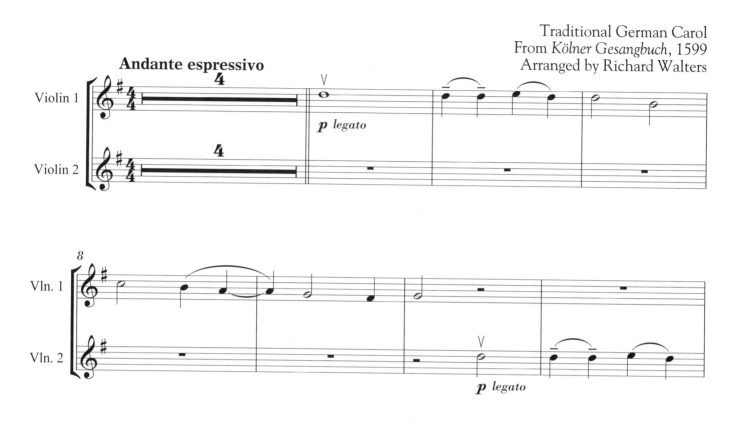

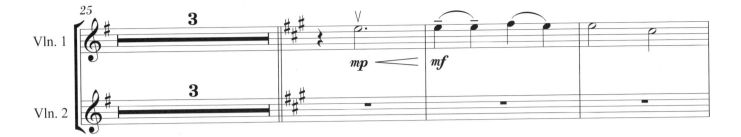

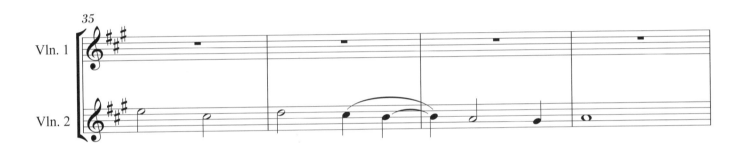

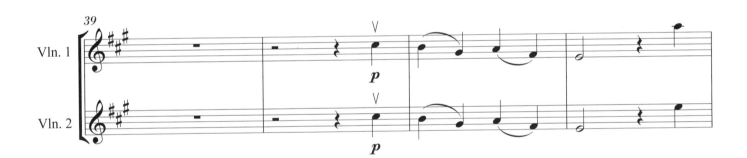

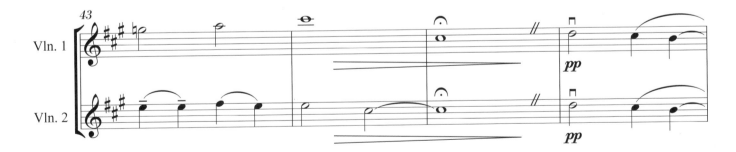

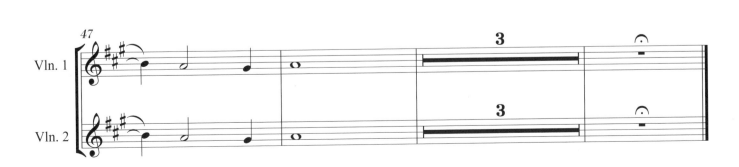

O Come, All Ye Faithful
(Adeste Fideles)

John Francis Wade
Arranged by Joshua Parman

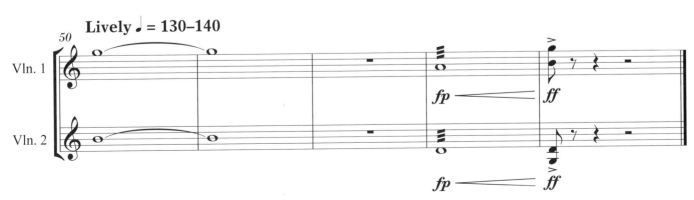

O Come, O Come Emmanuel

French Melody, 15th century
Arranged by Richard Walters

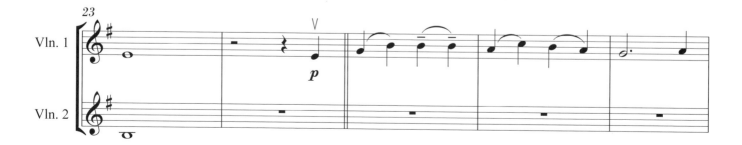

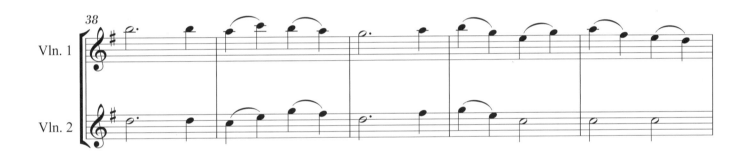

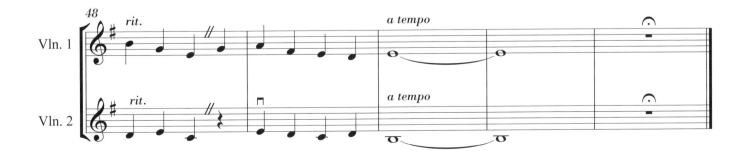

O Holy Night

Adolphe Adam
Transcribed by Celeste Avery

Andante maestoso

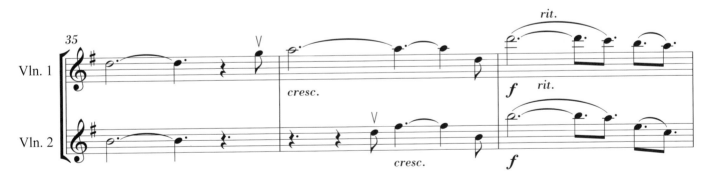

Still, Still, Still

Traditional Austrian Carol
Adapted from an arrangement
by Brian Dean

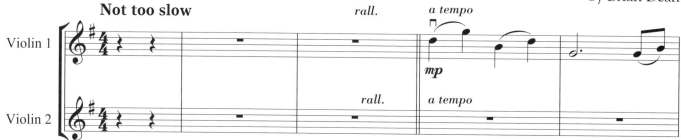

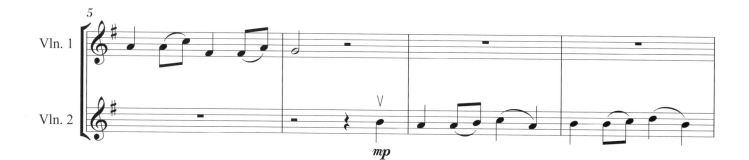

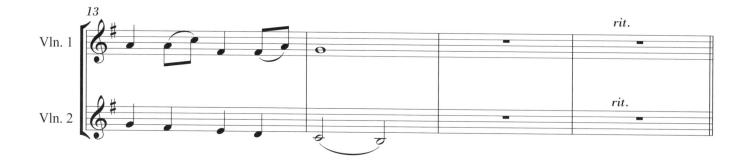

What Child Is This?

16th century English Folksong
Adapted from an arrangement
by Bryan Stanley

Slower

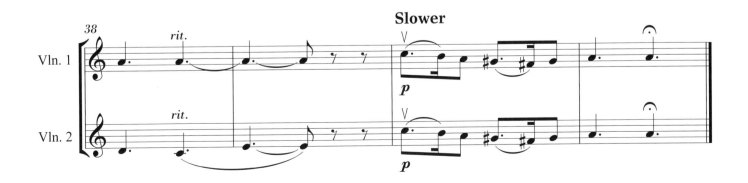

Silent Night

Franz X. Gruber
Arranged by Brendan Fox

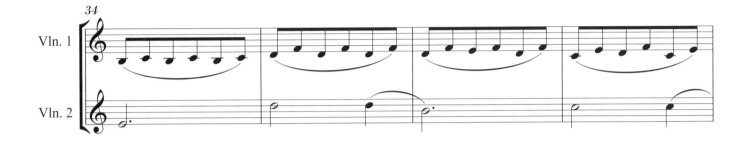

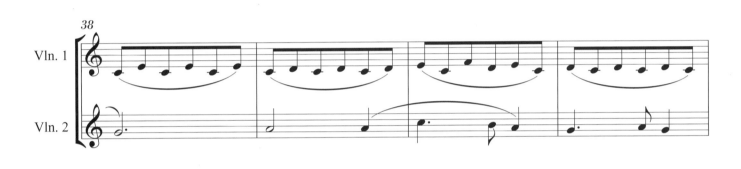

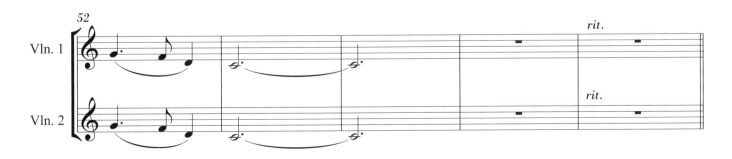

Hushed and still

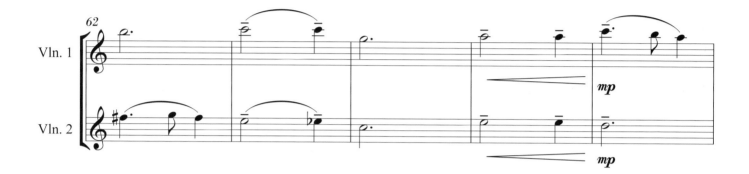

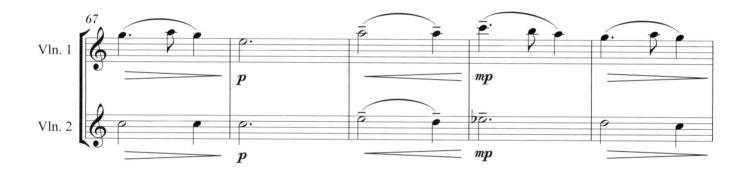

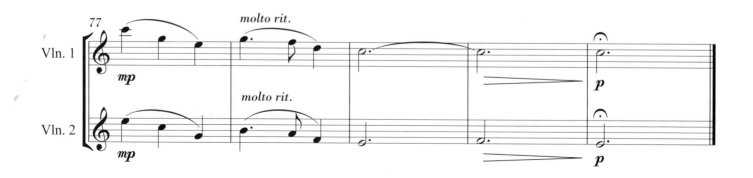